THE GREAT CELLO SOLOS

SELECTED & EDITED BY

JULIAN LLOYD WEBBER

The purpose of this collection is to bring the essential short pieces for the cello together in one attractive volume.
Great care has been taken to make use of the composers' original editions, and editorial markings have, I trust, been kept to a helpful minimum.

I hope that *The Great Cello Solos* will give much pleasure to players and listeners alike. - J. L.W.

Exclusive distributors:
Hal Leonard Europe Limited
Distribution Centre
Newmarket Road, Bury St Edmunds Suffolk, IP33 3YB
www.halleonard.com

PIANO ACCOMPANIMENT

CHESTER MUSIC

JULIAN LLOYD WEBBER

Since completing his studies in Geneva with Pierre Fournier, Julian Lloyd Webber has performed throughout the world, partnering many of the great orchestras and musicians of our time. Recent engagements include appearances with the Berlin Philharmonic Orchestra under Lorin Maazel, the Czech Philharmonic Orchestra under Vaclav Neumann, the Royal Philharmonic Orchestra under Sir Yehudi Menuhin and performances at the Sydney Opera House, the Konzerthaus in Vienna and the Kennedy Center in Washington, DC. He has toured the Far East, Australia, Europe, Scandinavia, the USA and Canada.

Since 1984 Julian Lloyd Webber has recorded for the Philips label. His performance of the Elgar Cello Concerto with the Royal Philharmonic Orchestra under Sir Yehudi Menuhin won the 1987 BPI award for the Best British Classical Recording. Other releases include the concertos of Dvořák, Haydn, Honegger and Saint-Saëns and the Britten and Shostakovich sonatas amongst others.

Julian Lloyd Webber has made first recordings of more than 25 works, including Malcolm Arnold's 'Fantasy', Frank Bridge's 'Oration' (Concerto elegaico), Britten's 'Suite No.3', Holst's 'Invocation', Vaughan Williams' 'Fantasia on Sussex Folk Tunes', Andrew Lloyd Webber's 'Variations', Rodrigo's 'Concierto como un divertimento' and Sir Arthur Sullivan's 'Concerto'.

Notes on the pieces:

ALLEGRO APPASSIONATO: SAINT-SAËNS

A composition which is in every cellist's repertoire, and rightly so for its enthusiasm drives on from first note to last.

APRÈS UN RÊVE: FAURÉ

This haunting melody is so well suited to the cello that it is today probably heard more often than in its original song version,which was composed in 1865 to words by Bussine.

ARIOSO: BACH

Although the Arioso is now famous as a cello solo, it began life as a piece for oboe with string accompaniment in Bach's Cantata No.156. Its sinuous melodic line is well suited to the cello.

ELÉGIE: FAURÉ

This masterpiece was composed in 1883. It is a beautiful work which shows Fauré's great gift for writing miniatures. The broad sweep of the main theme exploits the cello's elegiac qualities.

KOL NIDREI: BRUCH

Kol Nidrei is based on two Hebraic themes - one a heartfelt lament in the minor key, the other a celestial melody in the major. Bruch's lyrical writing for the cello is unsurpassed.

THE SWAN: SAINT-SAËNS

The Swan (Le Cygne) from Le Carnaval des Animaux is surely the most famous piece of music ever written for the cello. For many years it was the only piece from the work which Saint-Saëns would allow to be published separately.

SONG WITHOUT WORDS: MENDELSSOHN

This was Mendelssohn's very last composition, and it is not an arrangement of one of the famous Songs Without Words for piano but an original piece for cello and piano. Mendelssohn was obviously drawn to the cello as he had previously written two fine sonatas for the instrument. If only he had written a concerto!

ALLEGRO APPASSIONATO

Composed by Camille Saint-Saëns. Arranged by Julian Lloyd Webber.

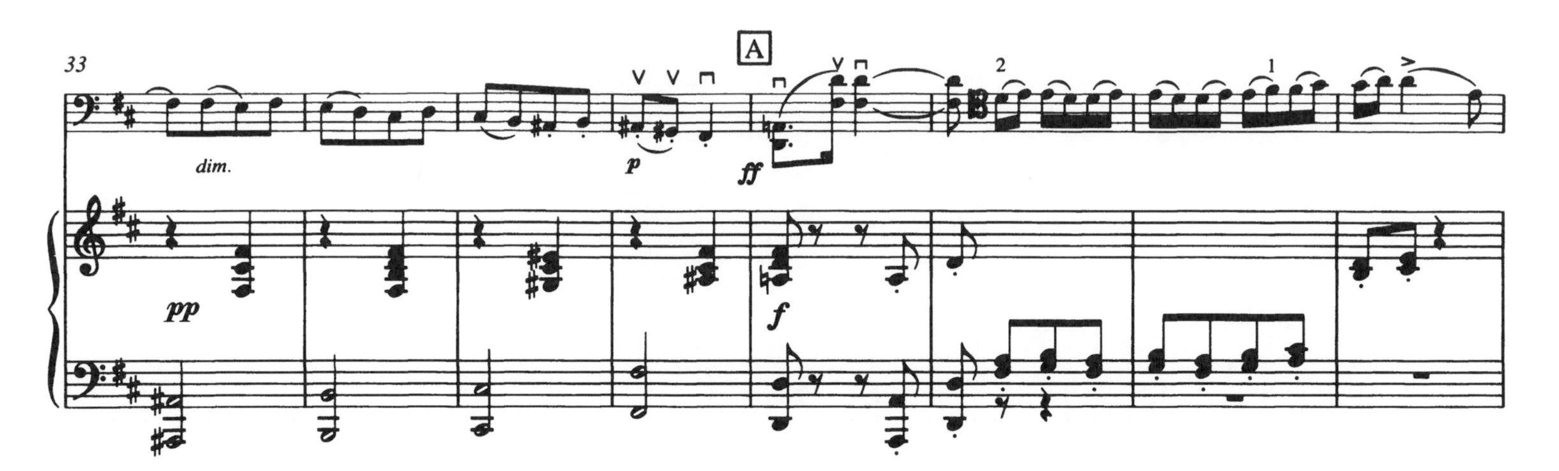
33
A
dim.
p
ff
pp
f
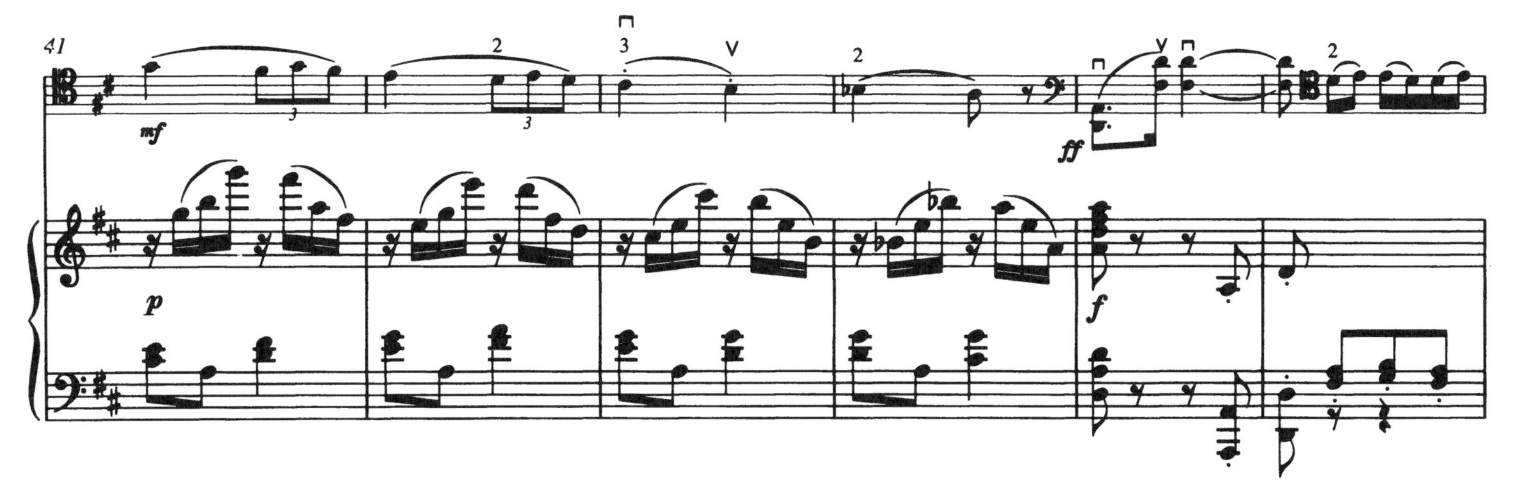
41
mf
p
ff
f

47
dim.
p

53
p

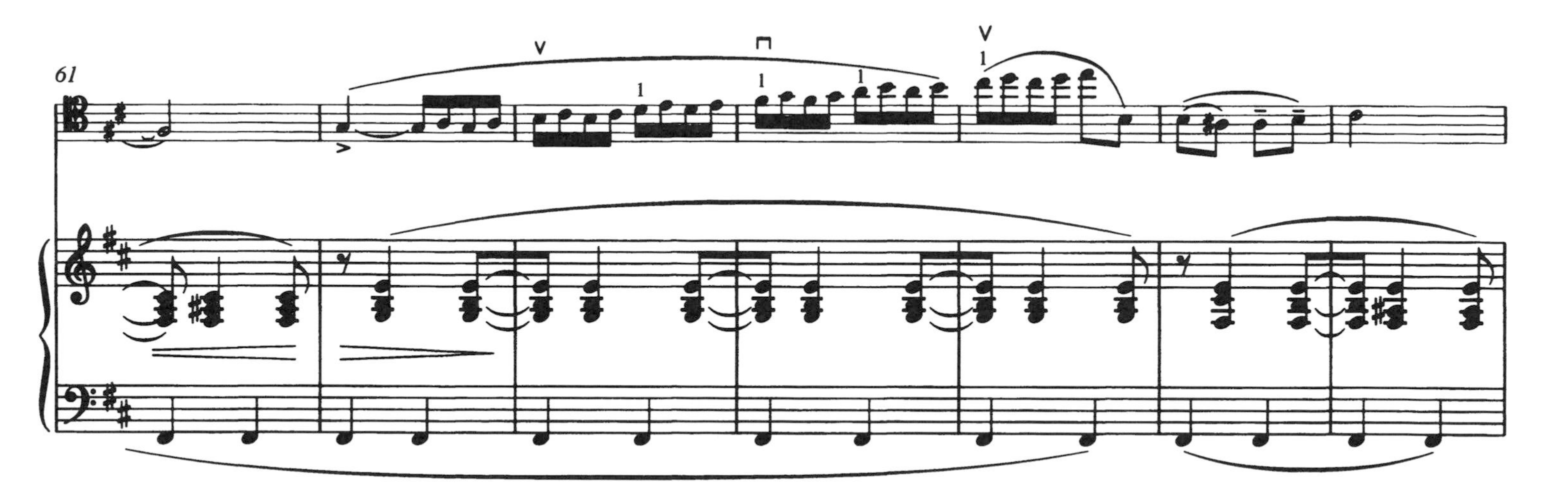
61

68
pp
più lento
string.
cresc.

76
a tempo
f dim.
p
colla parte

85
B
sempre p
p

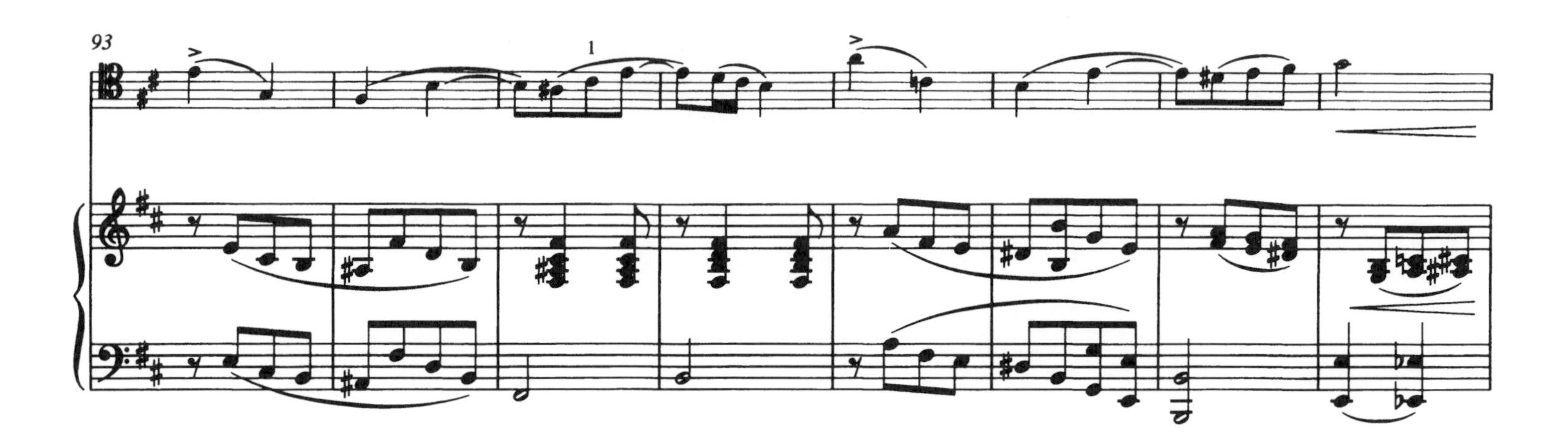
93
1

101

109
cresc.
dim.
C
ff

f

118
mf
p

124
ff
f
mf

130
dim.
p
dim.
p

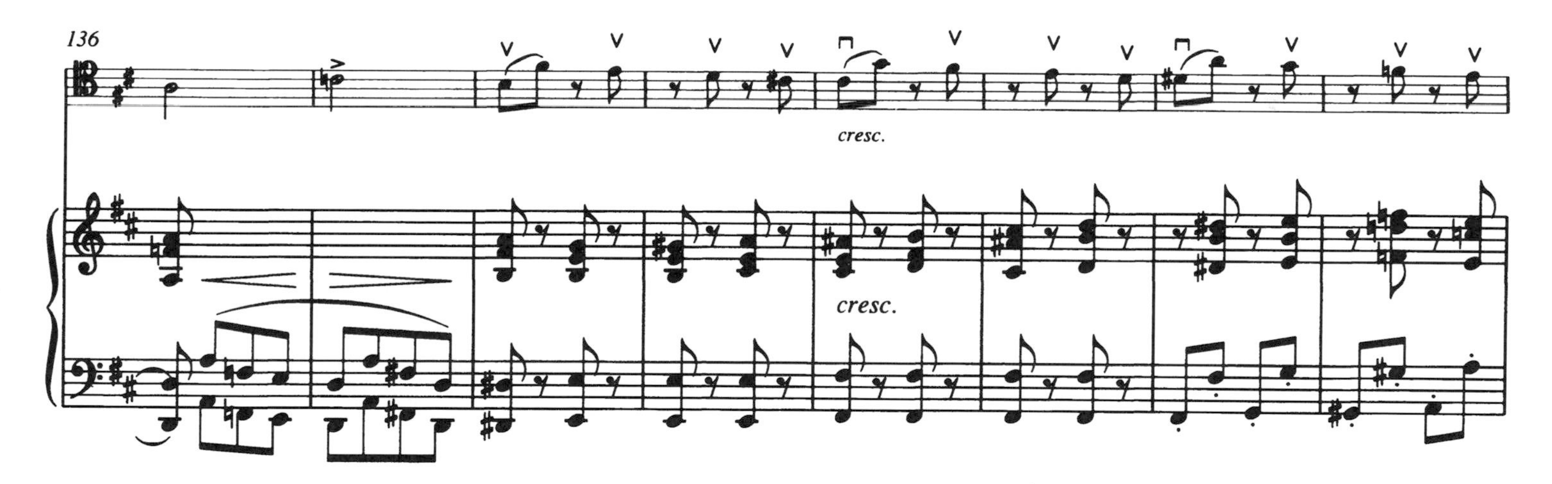
136
cresc.
cresc.

144
f
f

D
ff
p
cresc.
p leggiero
f

180
dim.
poco meno mosso
dolce
poco meno mosso
pp

187
a tempo
cresc.
a tempo
cresc.

196
f
f

203
ff
p
cresc.

209
ff

APRÈS UN RÊVE

Composed by Gabriel Fauré. Arranged by Julian Lloyd Webber.

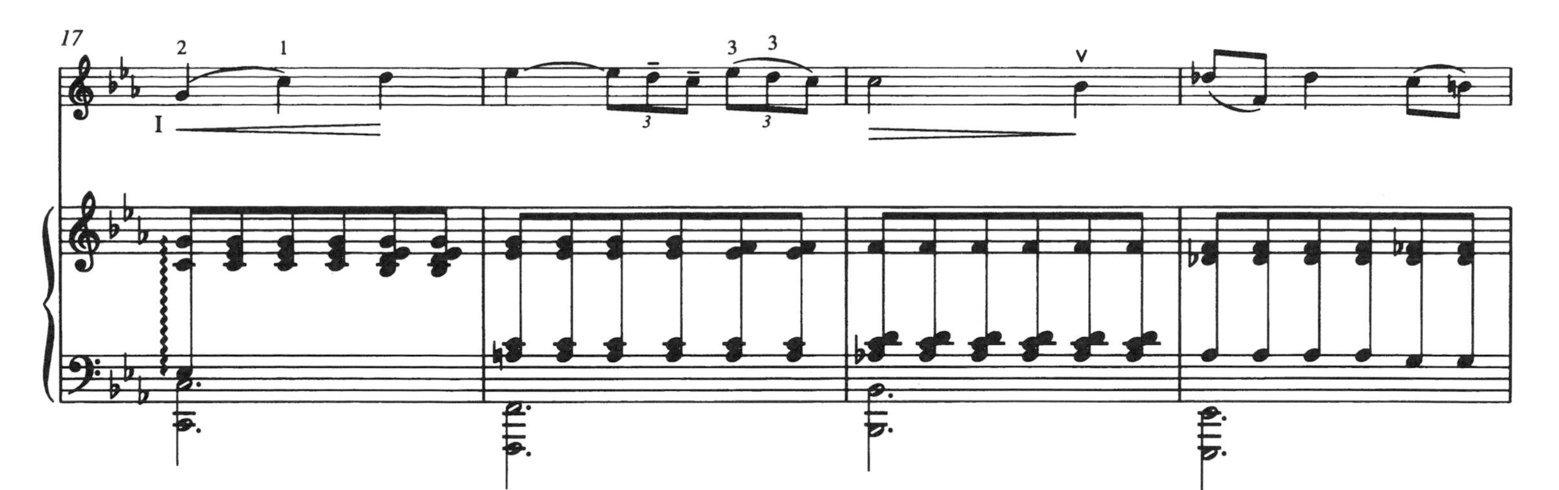
17
I

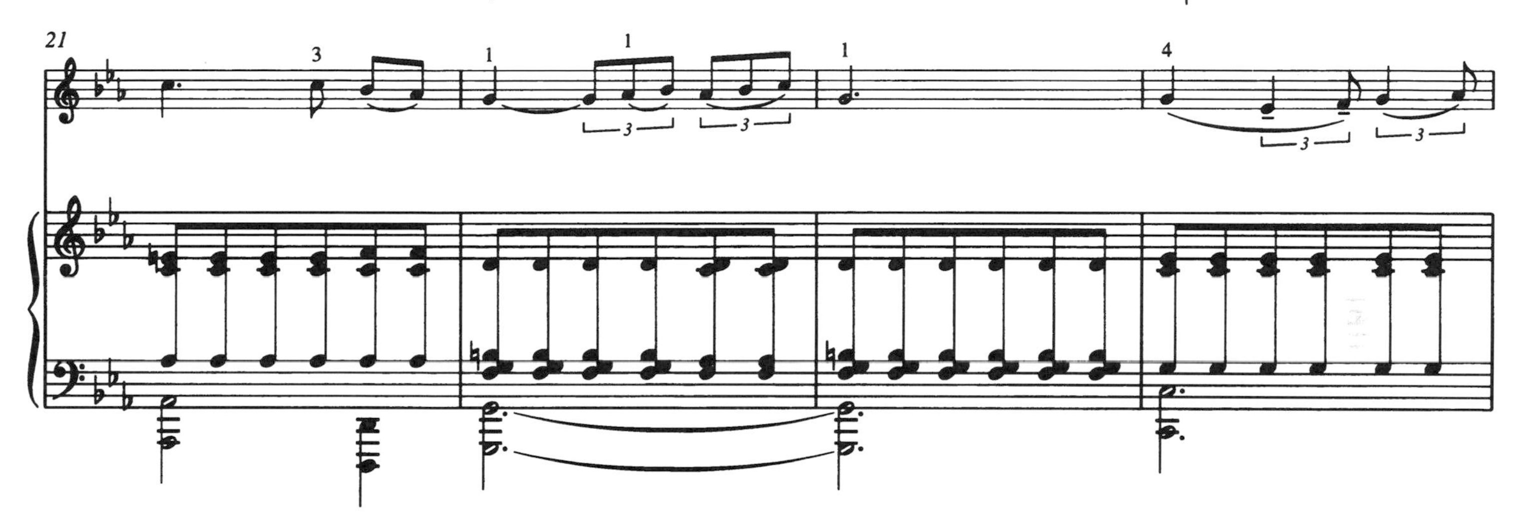
21

25
II
cresc. poco a poco
I

29
f

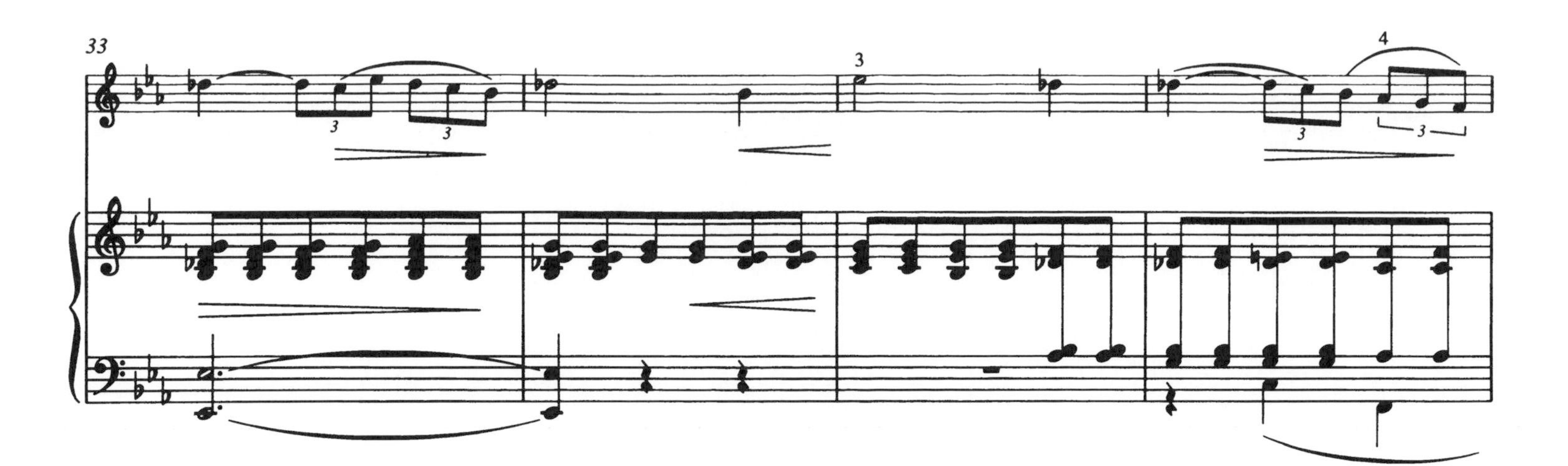
33
3
4

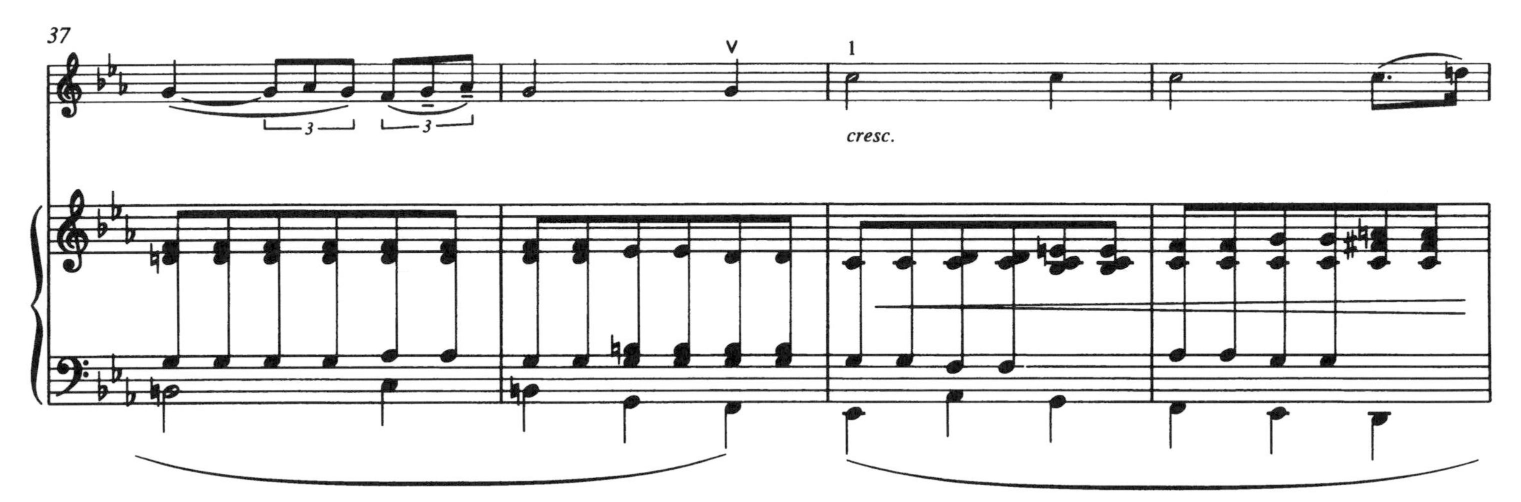
37
1
cresc.

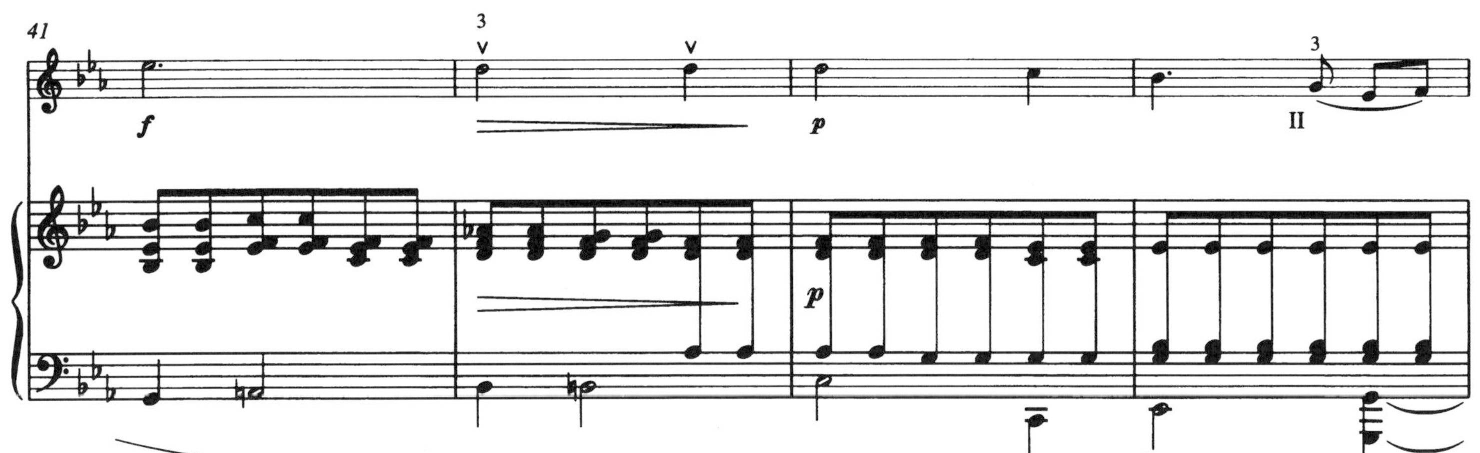
41
f
3
p
3
II
p

45
pp
2
2
III
pp
8va basso

ARIOSO

Composed by Johann Sebastian Bach. Arranged by Julian Lloyd Webber.

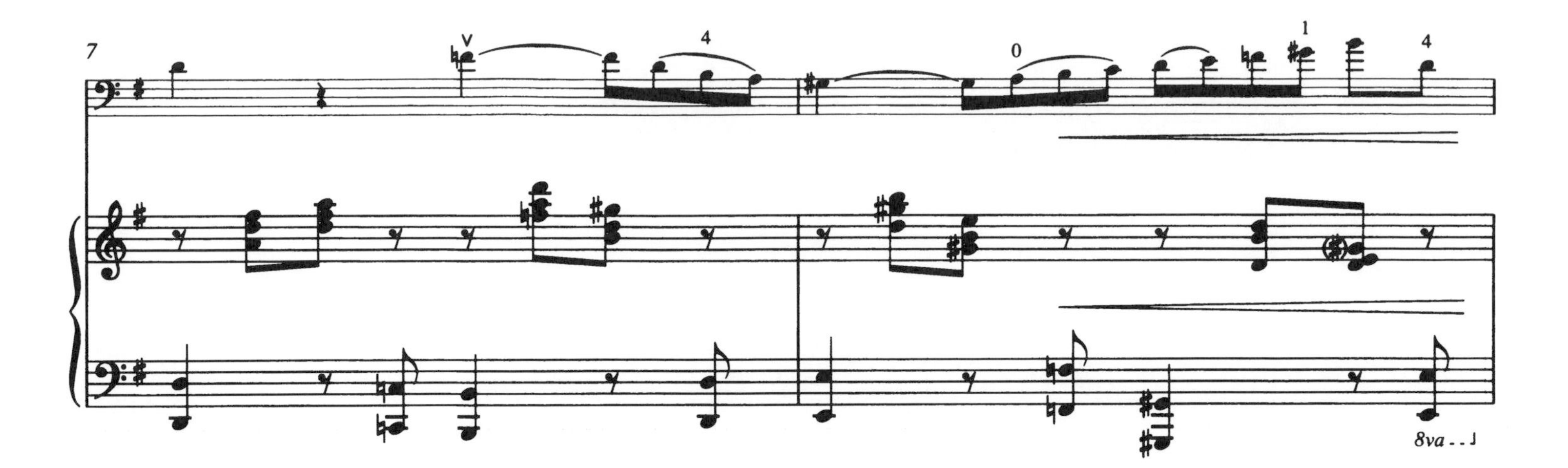
7
8va

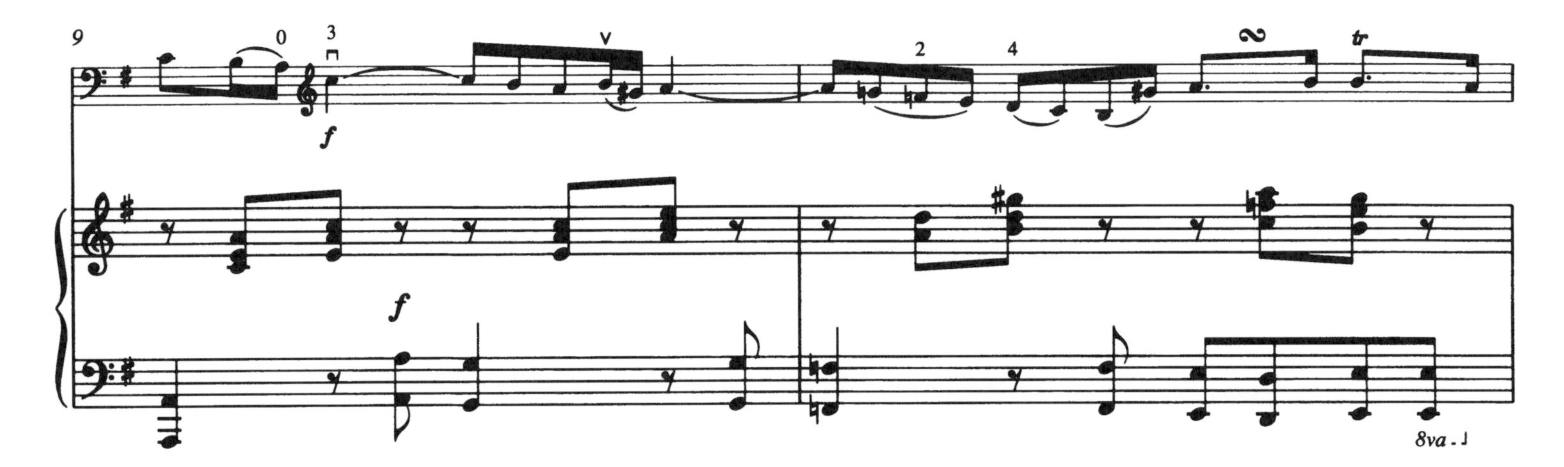
9
f
f
tr
8va

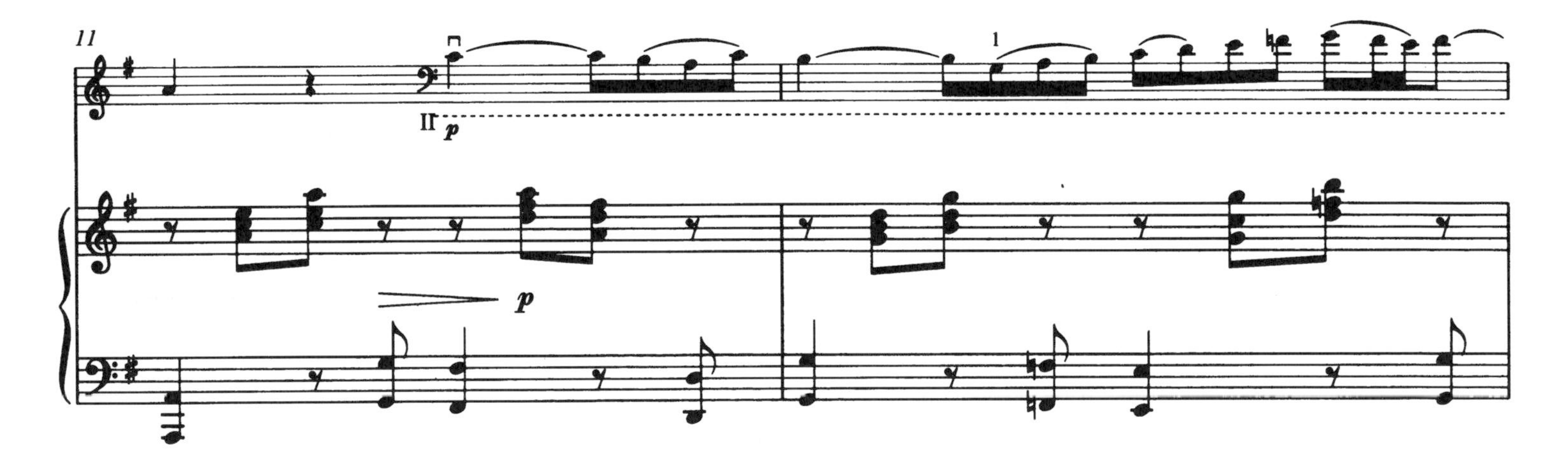
11
II p
p

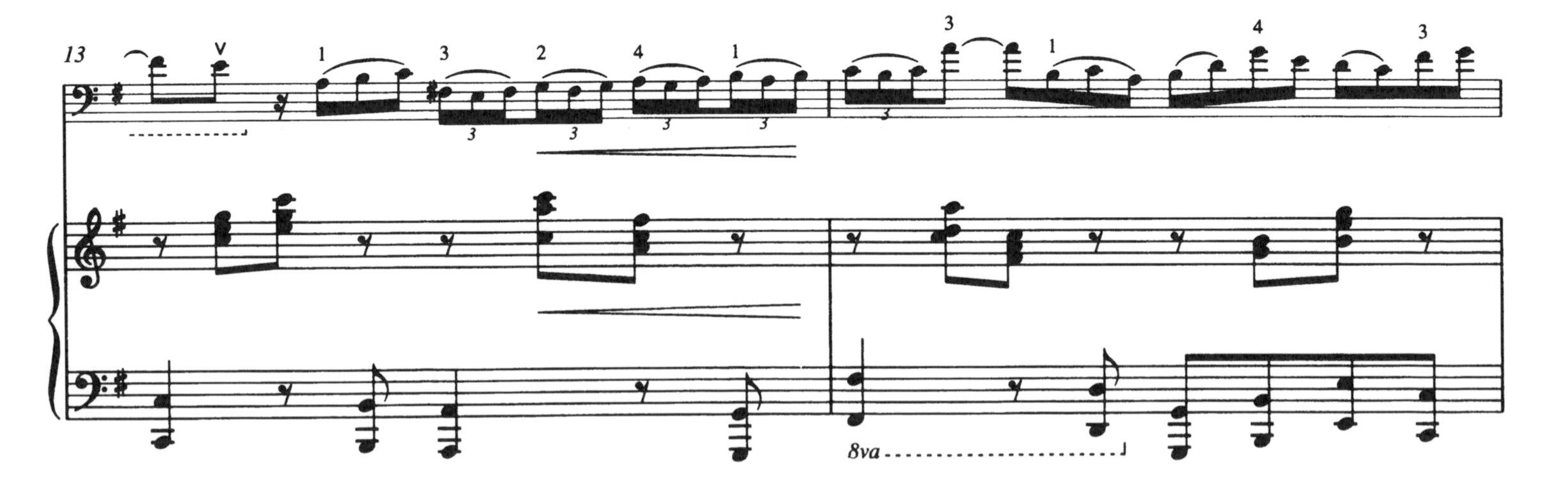
13
8va

15
II pp
pp

17
II

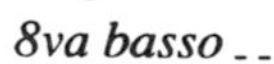
8va basso

19
tr
IV
(8va)

ELÉGIE

Composed by Gabriel Fauré. Arranged by Julian Lloyd Webber.

15
molto cresc.
ff
II ppp
f
dolcissimo
legato

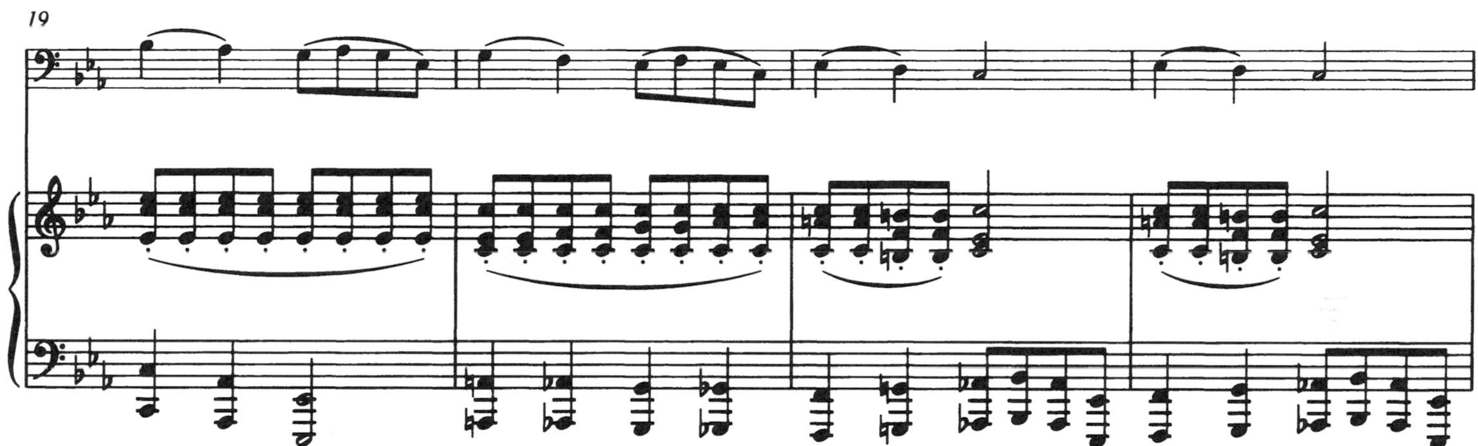
19

23
A
(sempre molto adagio)
pp
(sempre molto adagio)
cantabile espressivo
pp

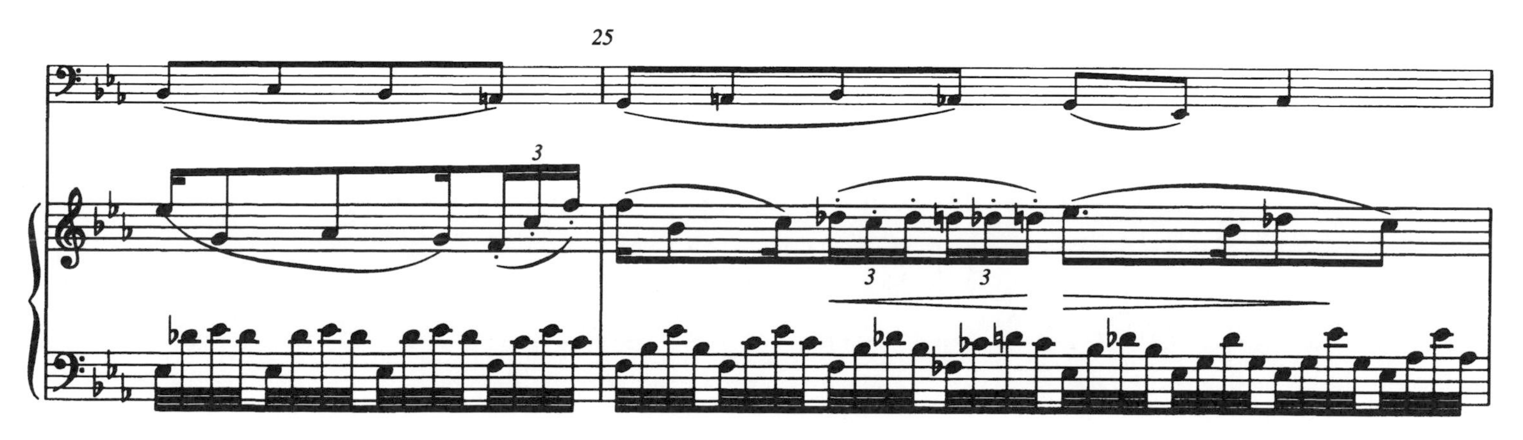
25

26
espressivo

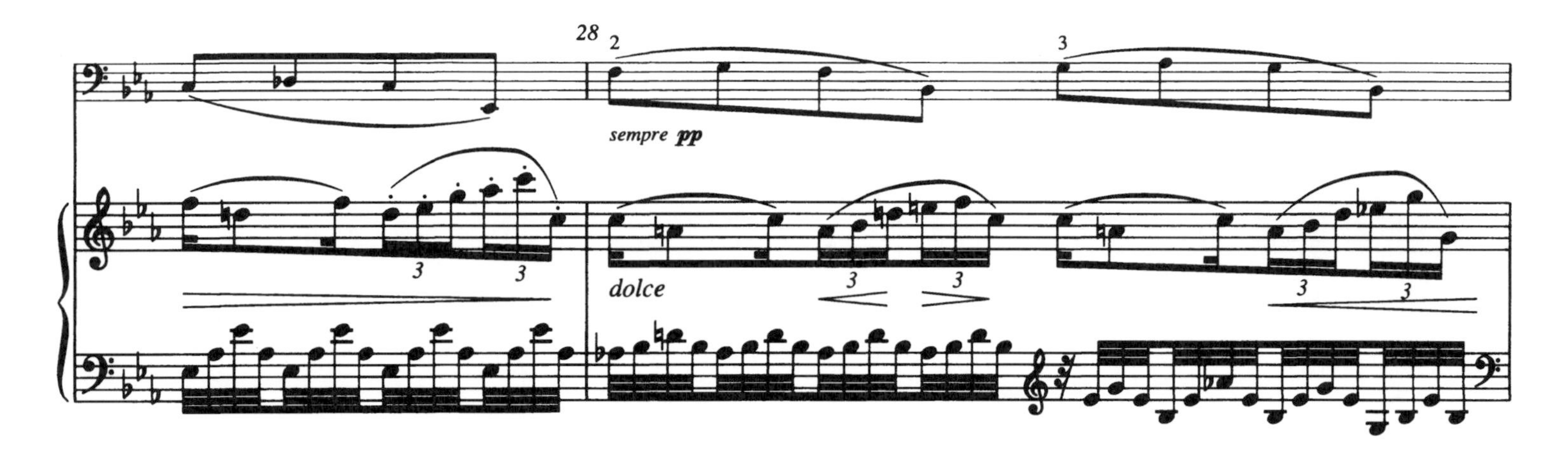
28
sempre pp
dolce

29
poco rit.
a tempo
espressivo
poco rit.
a tempo
pp
legato

31

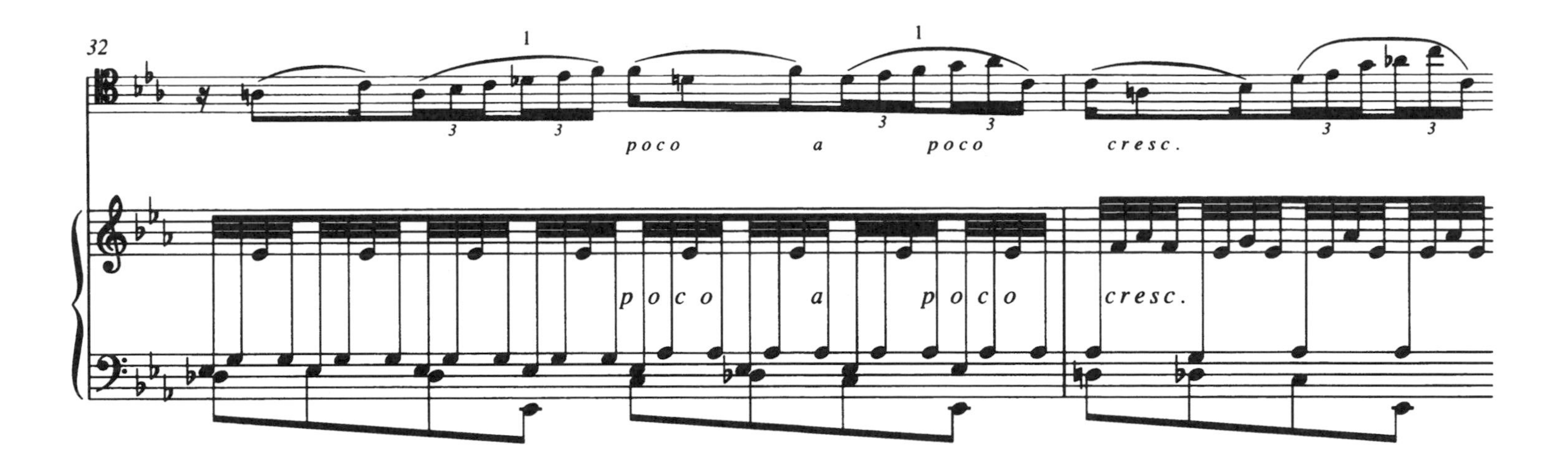
32
poco a poco cresc.
poco a poco cresc.

34
f
f
Ped. *
Ped. *

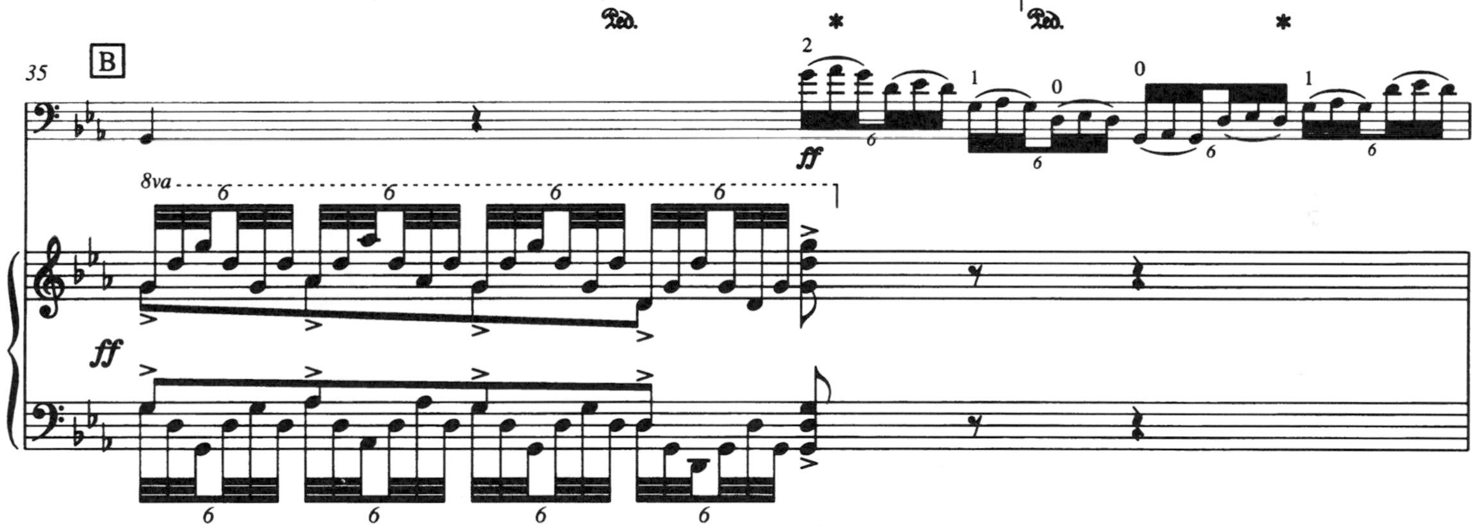
35
B
ff
8va
ff

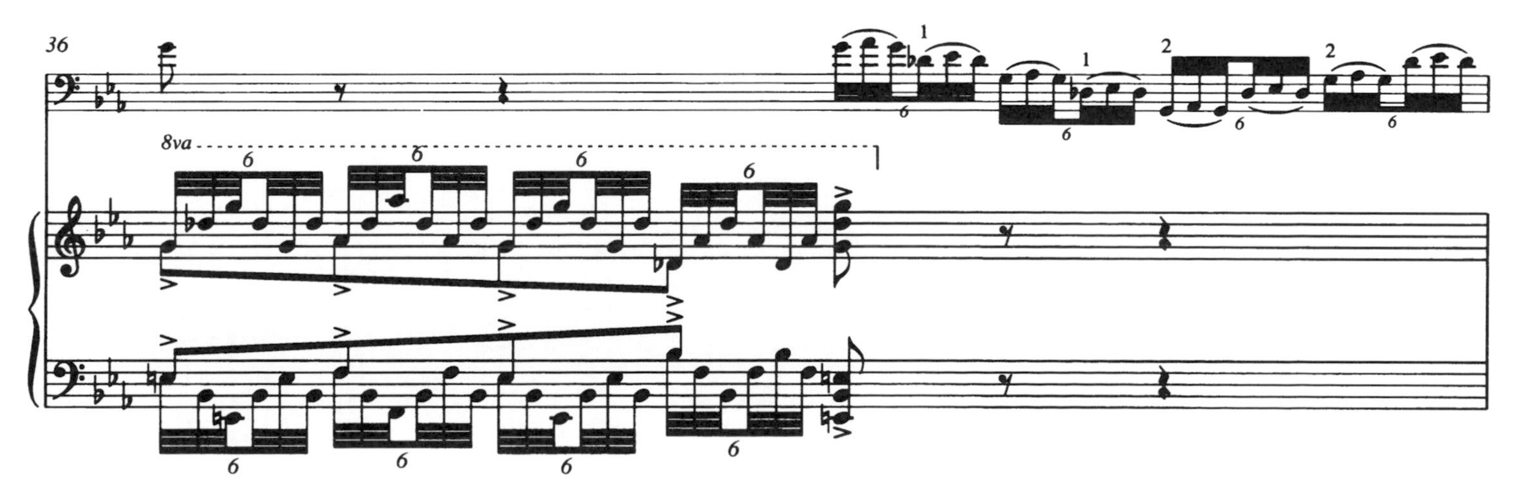
36
8va

37
8va
38
poco rit.
poco rit.
a tempo
39
ff
a tempo
sim.
ff
40

THE GREAT CELLO SOLOS

SELECTED & EDITED BY
JULIAN LLOYD WEBBER

The purpose of this collection is to bring the essential short pieces for the cello together in one attractive volume.
Great care has been taken to make use of the composers' original editions, and editorial markings have, I trust, been kept to a helpful minimum.

I hope that *The Great Cello Solos* will give much pleasure to players and listeners alike. - J. L.W.

Exclusive distributors:
Hal Leonard Europe Limited
Distribution Centre
Newmarket Road, Bury St Edmunds Suffolk, IP33 3YB
www.halleonard.com

CHESTER MUSIC

JULIAN LLOYD WEBBER

Since completing his studies in Geneva with Pierre Fournier, Julian Lloyd Webber has performed throughout the world, partnering many of the great orchestras and musicians of our time. Recent engagements include appearances with the Berlin Philharmonic Orchestra under Lorin Maazel, the Czech Philharmonic Orchestra under Vaclav Neumann, the Royal Philharmonic Orchestra under Sir Yehudi Menuhin and performances at the Sydney Opera House, the Konzerthaus in Vienna and the Kennedy Center in Washington, DC. He has toured the Far East, Australia, Europe, Scandinavia, the USA and Canada.

Since 1984 Julian Lloyd Webber has recorded for the Philips label. His performance of the Elgar Cello Concerto with the Royal Philharmonic Orchestra under Sir Yehudi Menuhin won the 1987 BPI award for the Best British Classical Recording. Other releases include the concertos of Dvořák, Haydn, Honegger and Saint-Saëns and the Britten and Shostakovich sonatas amongst others.

Julian Lloyd Webber has made first recordings of more than 25 works, including Malcolm Arnold's 'Fantasy', Frank Bridge's 'Oration' (Concerto elegaico), Britten's 'Suite No.3', Holst's 'Invocation', Vaughan Williams' 'Fantasia on Sussex Folk Tunes', Andrew Lloyd Webber's 'Variations', Rodrigo's 'Concierto como un divertimento' and Sir Arthur Sullivan's 'Concerto'.

Notes on the pieces:

ALLEGRO APPASSIONATO: SAINT-SAËNS

A composition which is in every cellist's repertoire, and rightly so for its enthusiasm drives on from first note to last.

APRÈS UN RÊVE: FAURÉ

This haunting melody is so well suited to the cello that it is today probably heard more often than in its original song version,which was composed in 1865 to words by Bussine.

ARIOSO: BACH

Although the Arioso is now famous as a cello solo, it began life as a piece for oboe with string accompaniment in Bach's Cantata No.156. Its sinuous melodic line is well suited to the cello.

ELÉGIE: FAURÉ

This masterpiece was composed in 1883. It is a beautiful work which shows Fauré's great gift for writing miniatures. The broad sweep of the main theme exploits the cello's elegiac qualities.

KOL NIDREI: BRUCH

Kol Nidrei is based on two Hebraic themes - one a heartfelt lament in the minor key, the other a celestial melody in the major. Bruch's lyrical writing for the cello is unsurpassed.

THE SWAN: SAINT-SAËNS

The Swan (Le Cygne) from Le Carnaval des Animaux is surely the most famous piece of music ever written for the cello. For many years it was the only piece from the work which Saint-Saëns would allow to be published separately.

SONG WITHOUT WORDS: MENDELSSOHN

This was Mendelssohn's very last composition, and it is not an arrangement of one of the famous Songs Without Words for piano but an original piece for cello and piano. Mendelssohn was obviously drawn to the cello as he had previously written two fine sonatas for the instrument. If only he had written a concerto!

ALLEGRO APPASSIONATO

Composed by Camille Saint-Saëns. Arranged by Julian Lloyd Webber.

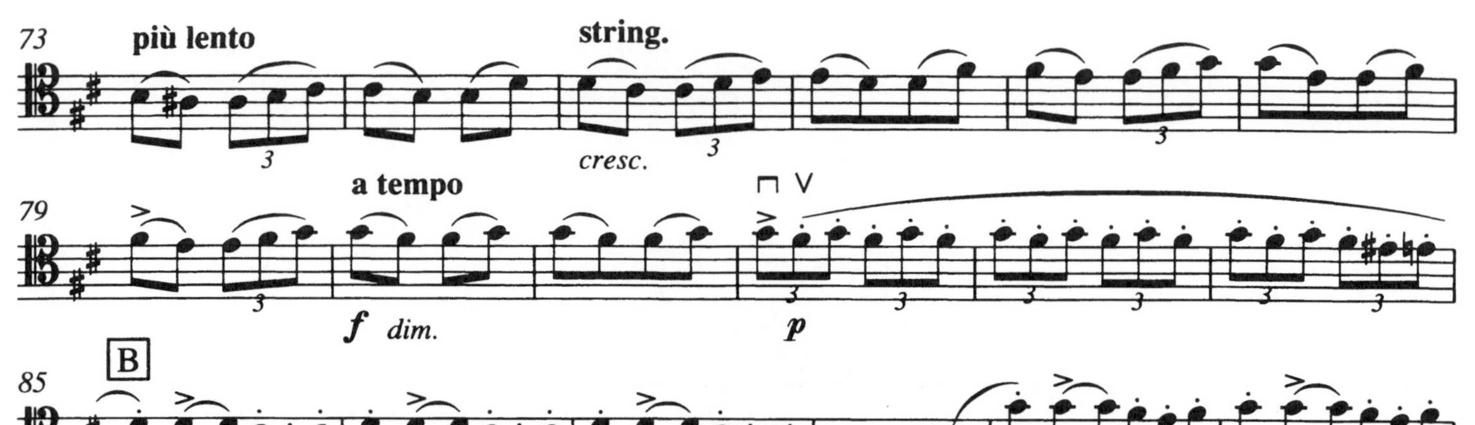
più lento
string.
cresc.
a tempo
dim.

B
sempre p

cresc.

dim.
C

dim.

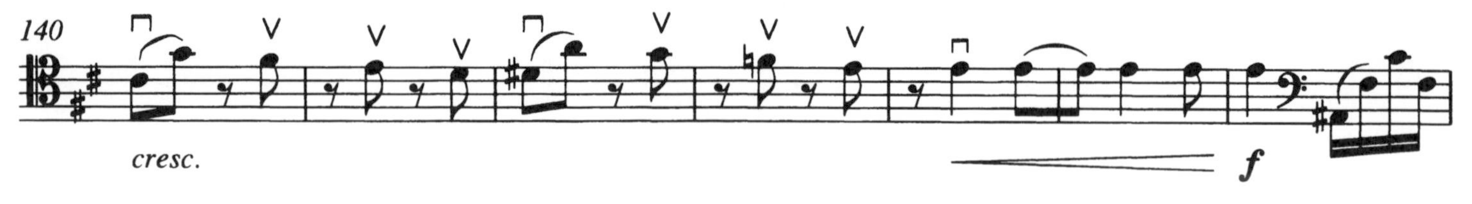
cresc.

D
p leggiero
p
dim.
poco meno mosso
dolce
a tempo
cresc.
f
ff

APRÈS UN RÊVE

Composed by Gabriel Fauré. Arranged by Julian Lloyd Webber.

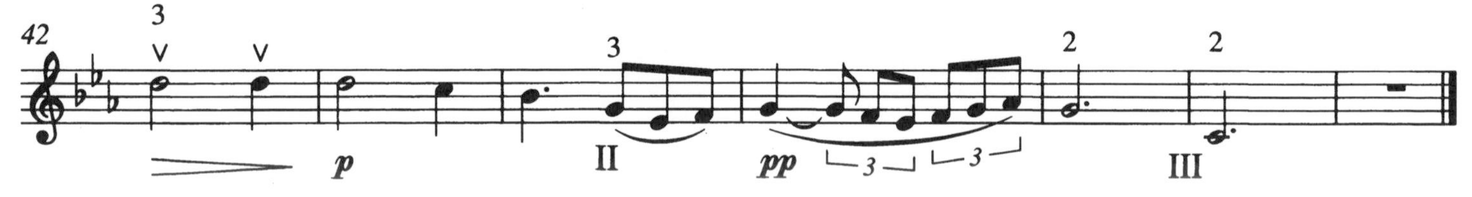

ARIOSO

Composed by Johann Sebastian Bach. Arranged by Julian Lloyd Webber.

ELÉGIE

Composed by Gabriel Fauré. Arranged by Julian Lloyd Webber.

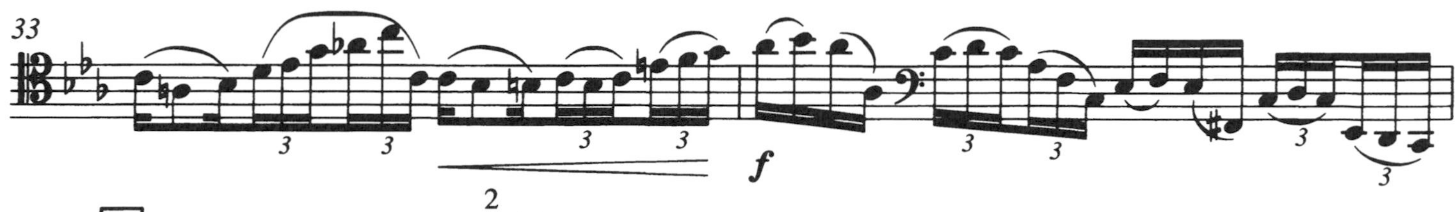
33
f

35
B
ff

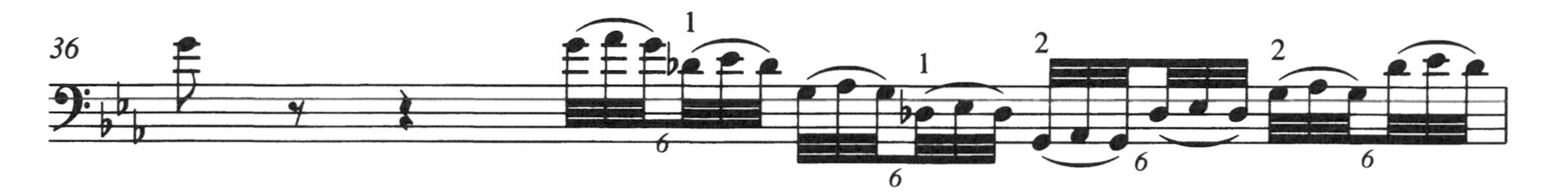
36

37

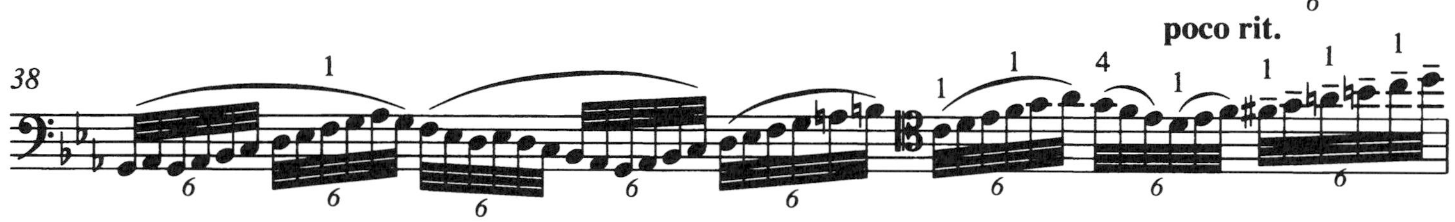
poco rit.
38

a tempo
39
ff

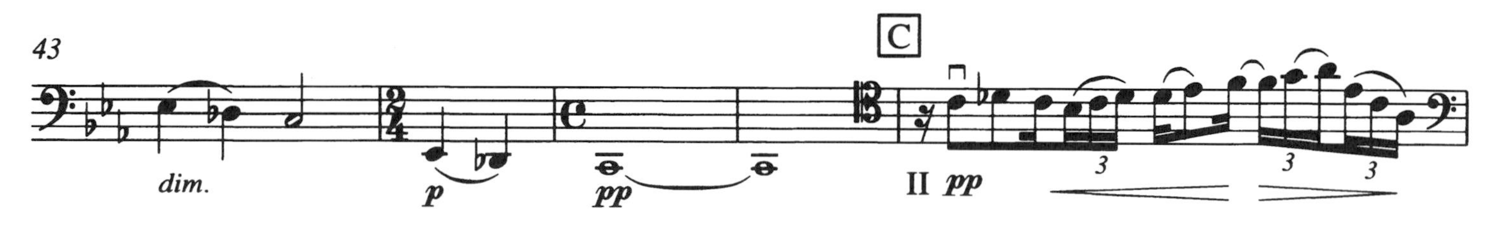
43
C
dim.
p
pp
II pp

48
sempre dim.

50
ppp

KOL NIDREI

Composed by Max Bruch. Arranged by Julian Lloyd Webber.

Un poco più animato
p dim.
dolce
cresc.
rit.
a tempo
poco
cresc.
tranquillo
morendo

SONG WITHOUT WORDS

Composed by Felix Mendelssohn. Arranged by Julian Lloyd Webber.

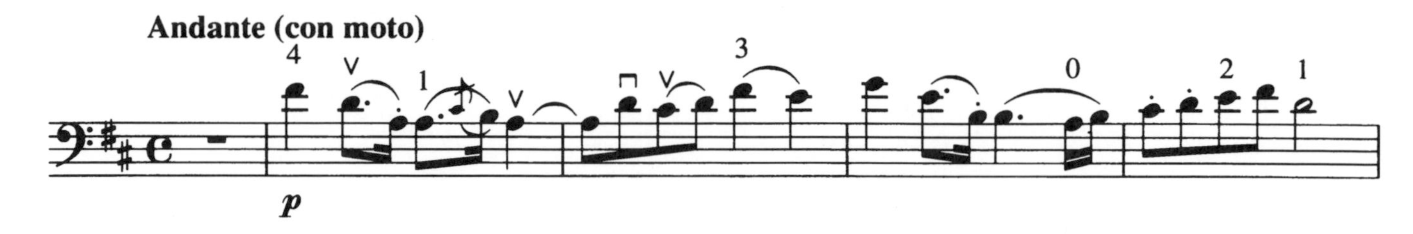

32
dim.
cresc.

36
C
cresc.
39

43
ritard.
dim.
II
tranquillo

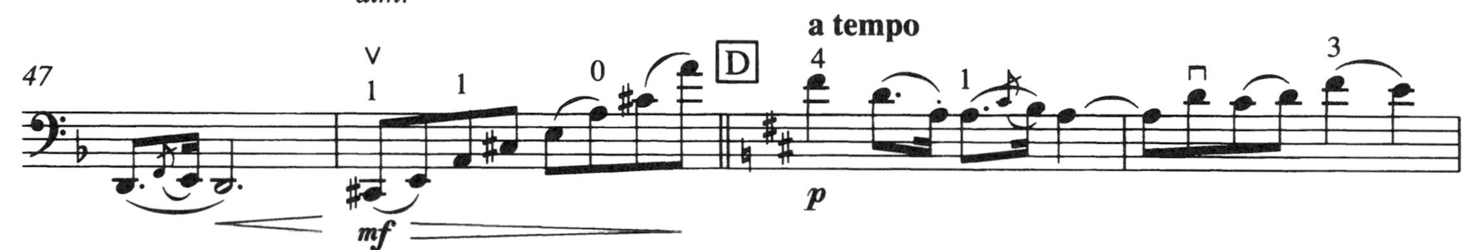
a tempo
47
D

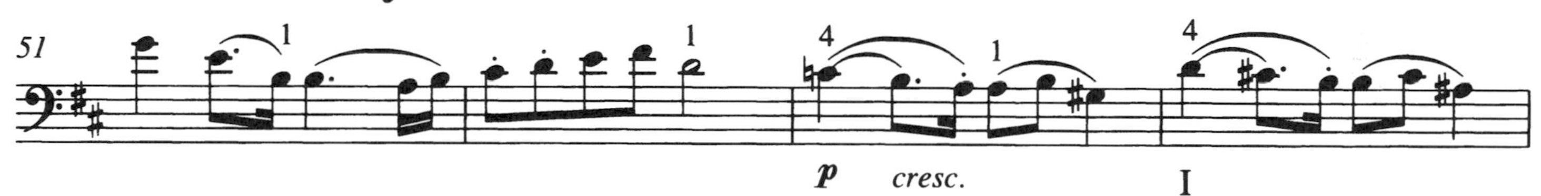
51
cresc.
I

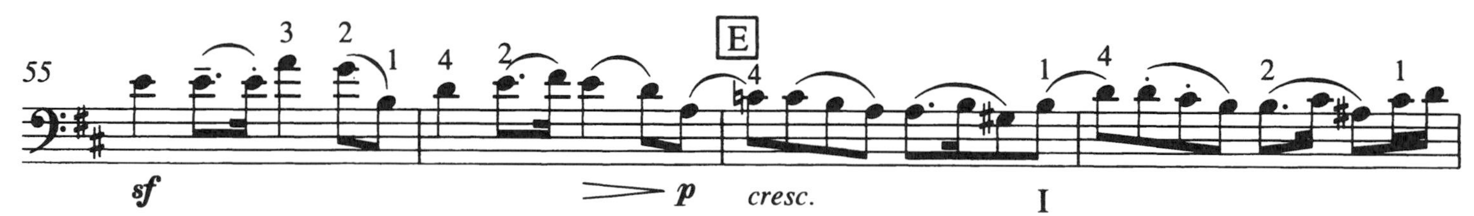
55
E
cresc.
I

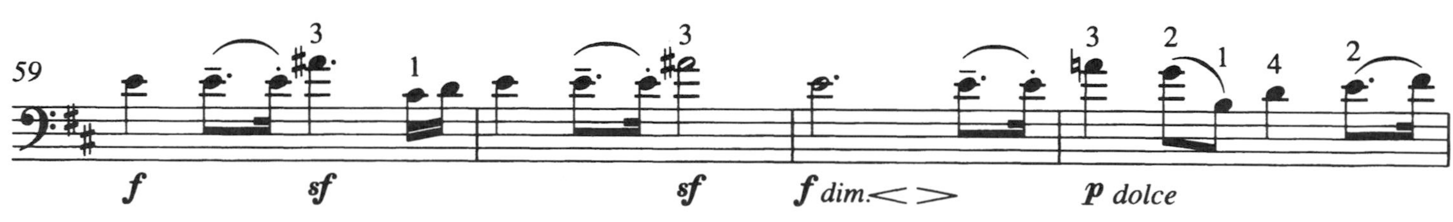
59
dim.
dolce

63
rit.
dim.

THE SWAN

Composed by Camille Saint-Saëns. Arranged by Julian Lloyd Webber.

* Although often marked 'Adagio' in arrangements, this is the marking in the full score.

41

42
6
sim.

43
dim.
dim.

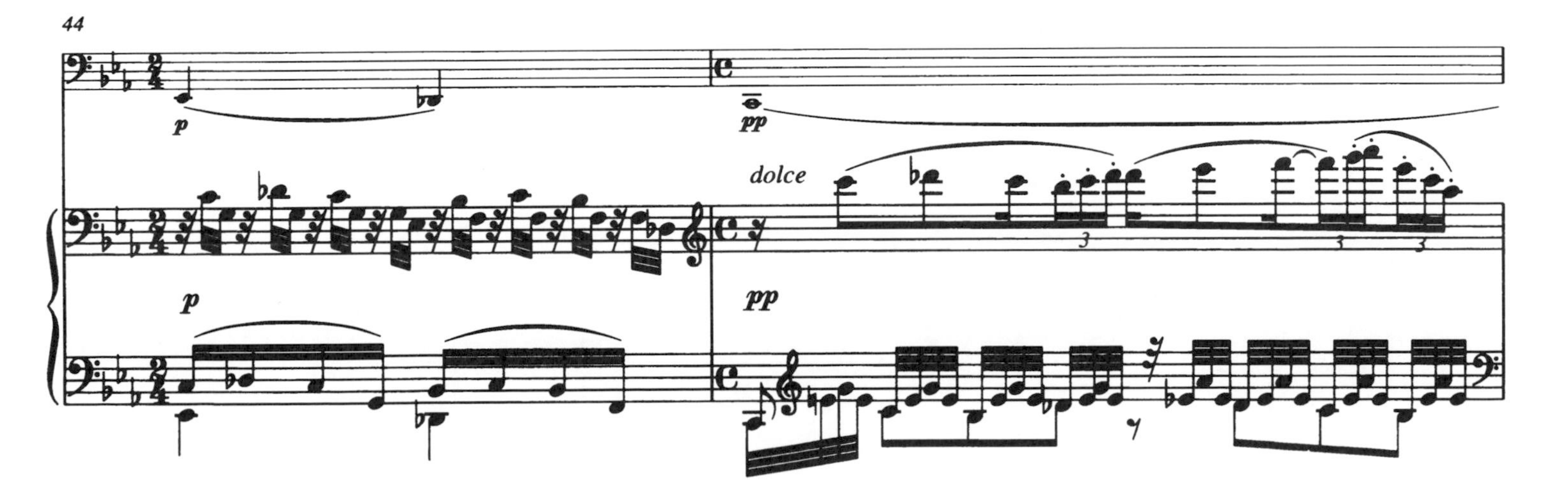
44
p
pp
dolce
p
pp

46
C
II pp
pp
3
3
3
3

48
3
3
3
3
3

49
sempre dim.
sempre dim.
ppp
ppp
1
3
3
3
3
3

3
51
dolcissimo
sempre
ppp

KOL NIDREI

Composed by Max Bruch. Arranged by Julian Lloyd Webber.

21
rfz
mf
p
ten.
p

26
B
cresc.
f
ten.
ten.
ten.
cresc.
pp
ff

31
p
p
ff
p

35
cresc.
p
cresc.
cresc.

C
con brio
fs
fp
dolce
p
p dolce
rfs
fp
D
espress.
tremolo
ten.
cresc.
rfs
L.H.
trem.
f
pp

57
E
Un poco più animato
p dim.
Un poco più animato
ten.
ten.
ten.
pp
pp sempre
6
6
6
6
Ped.
Ped.

60
Ped.
Ped.
Ped.
Ped.
Ped.
Ped.

62
Ped.
Ped.
Ped.

64
Ped.
Ped.
Ped.
Ped.
Ped.
Ped.

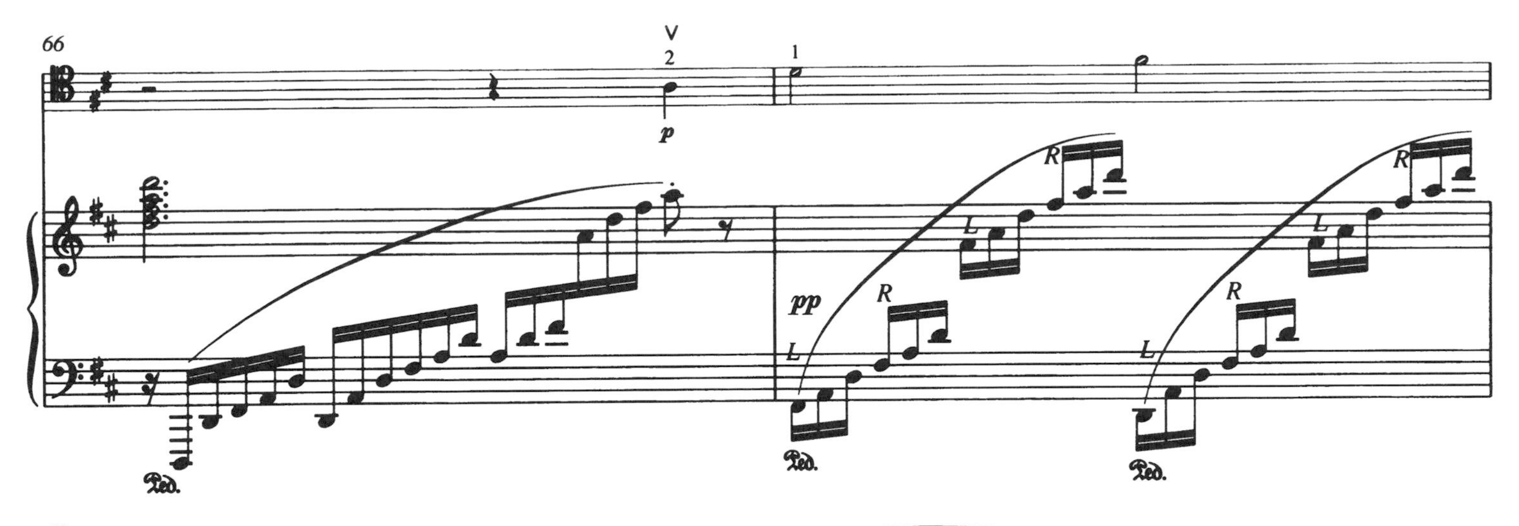
66
p
pp
L
R
Ped.

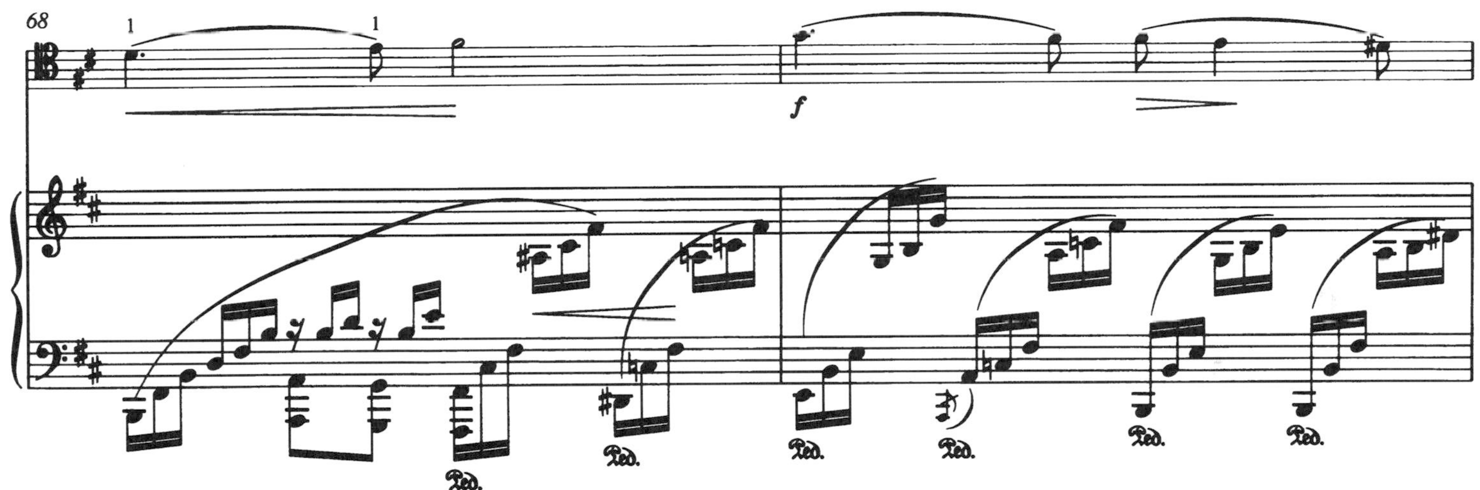
68
f
Ped.

70
dolce
cresc.
L
R
sim.
Ped.

73
F
f
p
Ped.

76
f
p
Ped.
Ped.

79
f
mf

p
Ped.
Ped.

82
f
dolce
pp

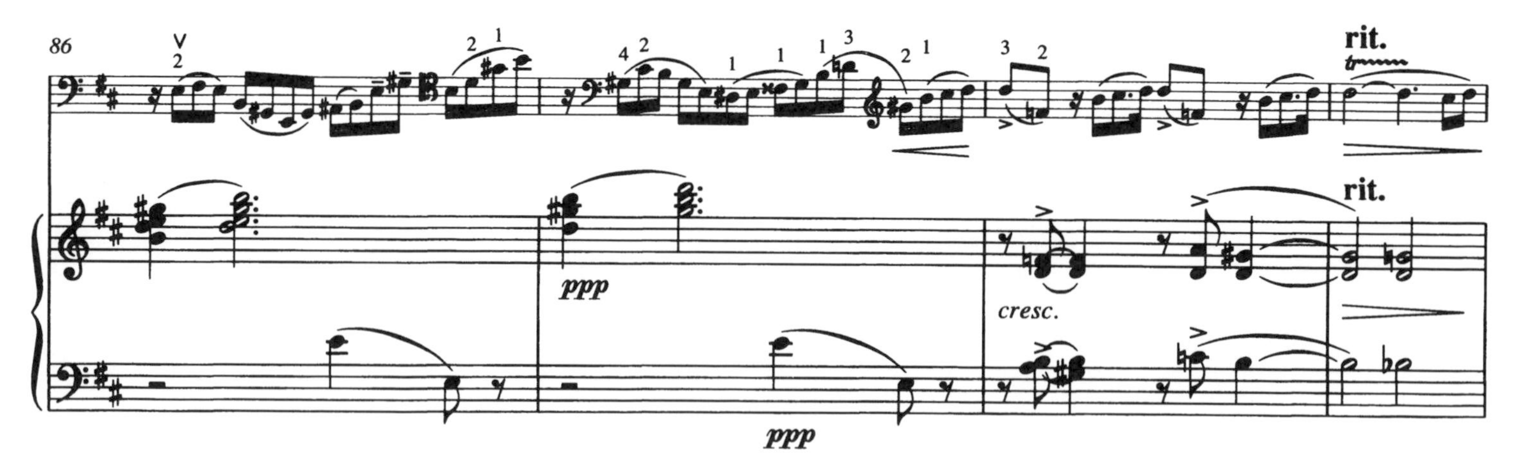
86
rit.
ppp
cresc.
rit.
ppp

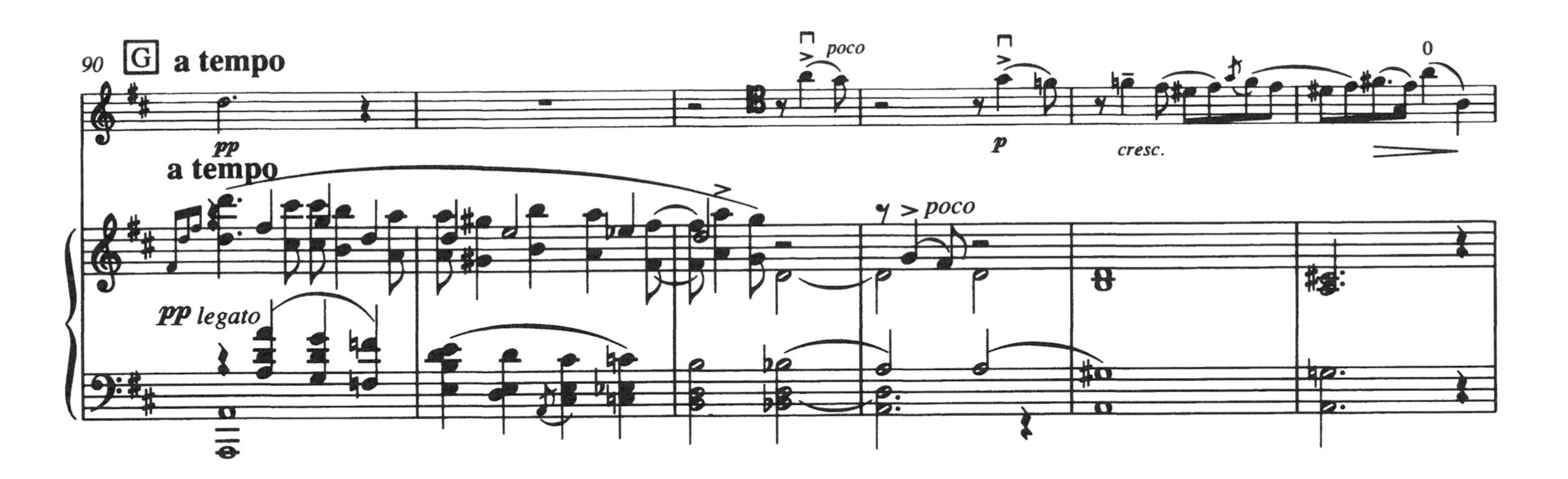
90
G
a tempo
poco
pp
p
cresc.
a tempo
poco
pp legato

96
pp
ten.
pp

101
H
ten.
p
pp

107
tranquillo
morendo
pp
ppp

SONG WITHOUT WORDS

Composed by Felix Mendelssohn. Arranged by Julian Lloyd Webber.

16
p
sf
mf
19
dim.
22
p
sf
26
B
mf agitato
cresc.
28
f
dim.

30
mf
cresc.
mf
cresc.

32
f
f

34
dim.
p
p
cresc.

dim.
p
cresc.

36
C
f
sf
p
cresc.
f
sf
p
cresc.

dim.

dim.

ritard.
II pp tranquillo

ritard.
pp tranquillo

D a tempo
49
p
a tempo
p

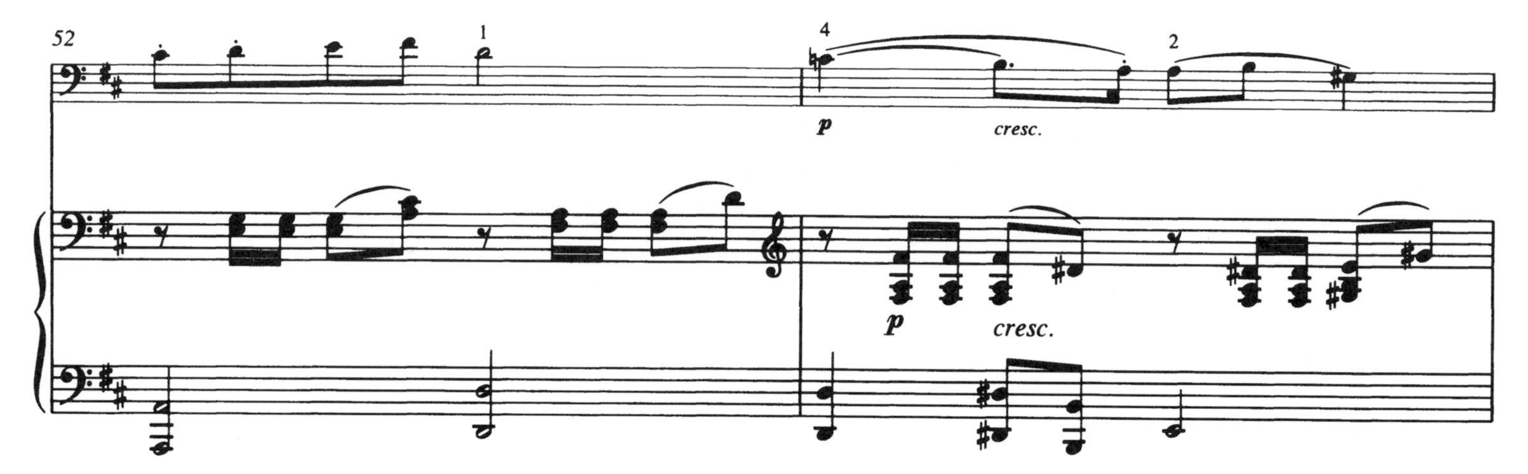
52
p
cresc.
p
cresc.

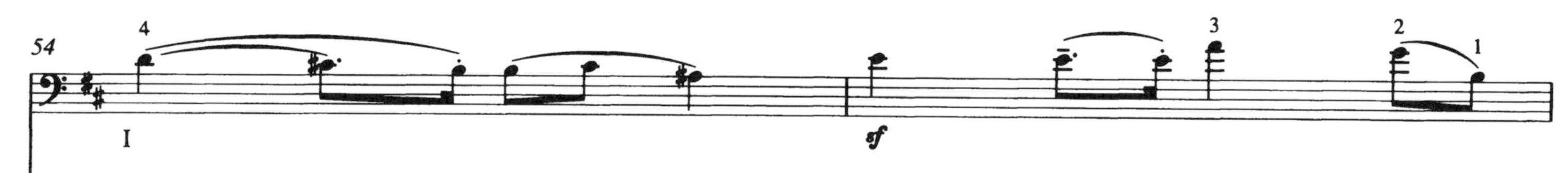
54
I
sf

p
sf

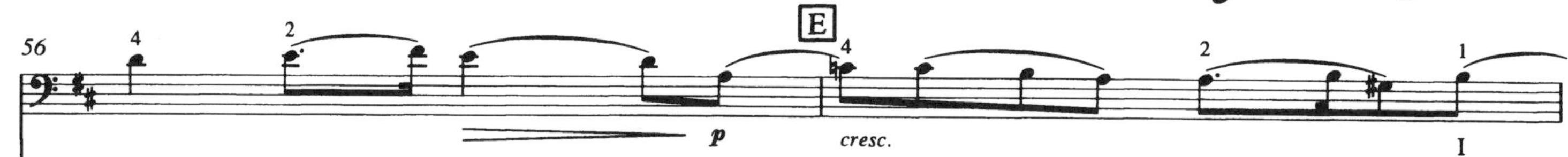
56
E
p
cresc.
I

cresc.

58
f
sf
f

60
sf
f dim.

f
dim.
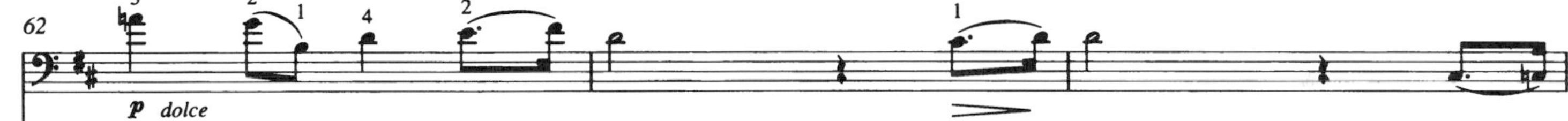
62
p dolce
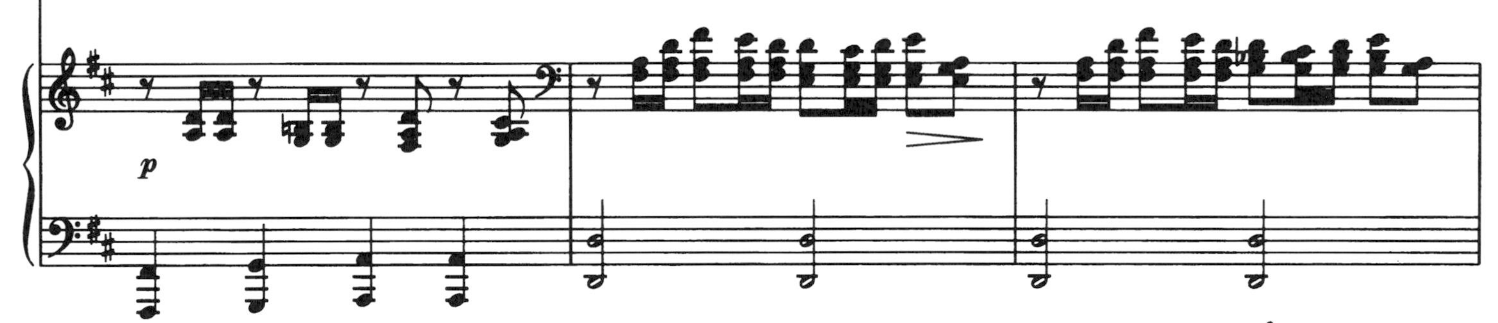
p

65
rit.
dim.
pp

rit.
dim.
pp

THE SWAN

Composed by Camille Saint-Saëns. Arranged by Julian Lloyd Webber.

* Although often marked 'Adagio' in arrangements,
this is the marking in the full score.

8
1
1
1
1

9
3

11
4

13

15

17
p
pp

19
0

21
mf
1

23
2
dim.

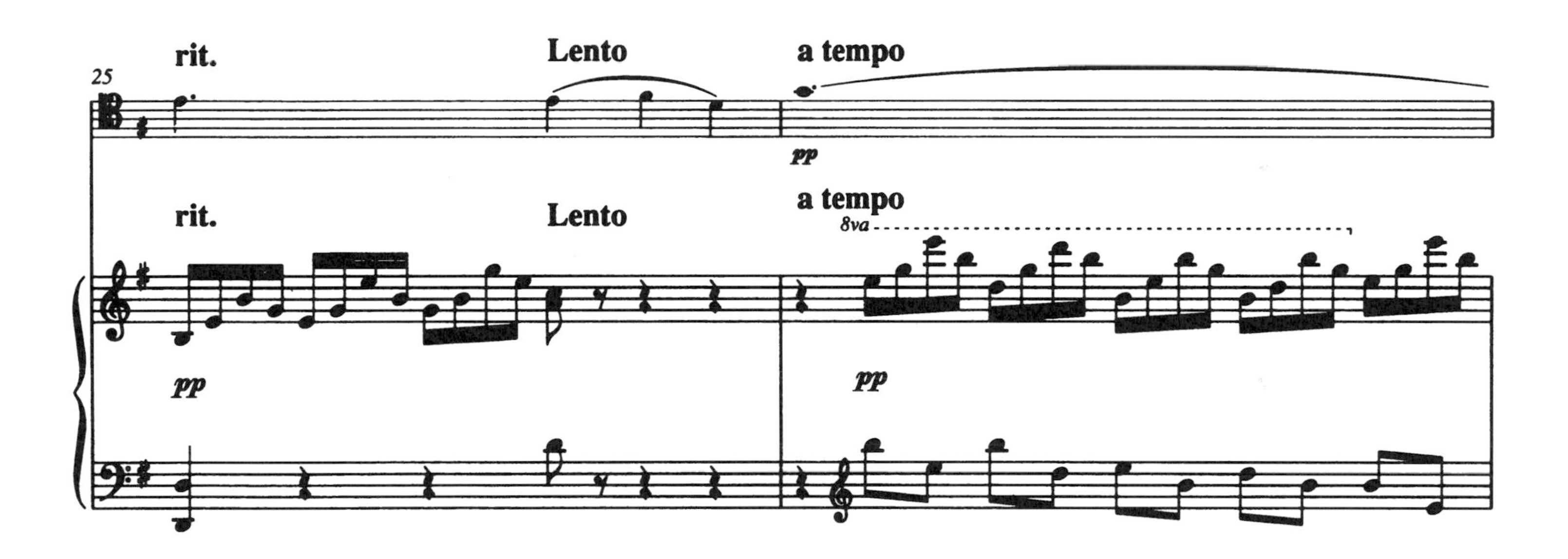
rit.
Lento
a tempo
25
pp
rit.
Lento
a tempo
8va
pp
pp

27
rit.